AN INTRODUCTION TO
POWERPOINT®
USING MICROSOFT® POWERPOINT® 2000

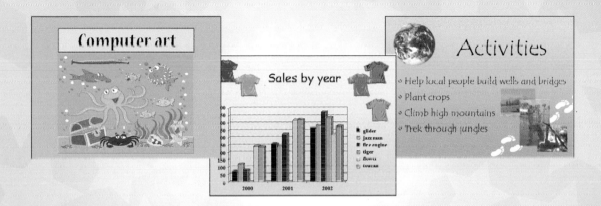

Ruth Brocklehurst

Designed by Isaac Quaye

Cover design by Zoe Wray
Edited by Rebecca Gilpin
Illustrated by Yann Brien
Photographs by Howard Allman
Technical consultant: Cathy Wickens

Contents

About this book

This book shows you how easy it is to create presentations using Microsoft® PowerPoint® 2000. There are examples of things you can do, all explained with simple step-by-step instructions.

It's a good idea to read this book from the beginning, as the later exercises build on basic skills you'll pick up on earlier pages. Once you've mastered the basics of PowerPoint, you can experiment with some of the other things it can do.

Extra help

ABSOLUTE BEGINNERS
Don't worry if you've never used a computer before. Pages 40-43 show you what equipment you need and how to load PowerPoint onto your computer.

STRANGE HAPPENINGS
If something unexpected happens, don't panic – the troubleshooting section on pages 44-46 helps you to deal with some common computer problems.

STRANGE WORDS
New computer words appear in bold lettering, **like this**. The glossary on page 47 explains these technical words in simple, everyday language.

I'm here to offer you advice and extra tips throughout the book.

About presentations

Giving a presentation is a way of telling an audience about ideas or information. Whether your audience is your class at school or people at work, you'll want to make your point clearly, in a way that interests them.

Microsoft® PowerPoint® 2000

PowerPoint 2000 is a computer **program** that helps you create lively presentations, that will grab the attention of any audience.

A PowerPoint presentation is made up of a series of pages on which you display information. The audience looks at these pages, either on a computer screen, or projected onto a wall.

You can give a PowerPoint presentation to a large audience, if you project it onto a large screen.

★ A guide to living in Space by Paul Mazunas ★

If you have access to the Internet, you can see some sample presentations on the Usborne Web site. Just go to **www.usborne-quicklinks.com** type the keyword "powerpoint" and follow the instructions on the screen.

PowerPoint® presentations

These pages show the different parts that make up a PowerPoint presentation. The individual pages of a presentation are called **slides**, so presentations are often called **slide shows**. In this book, you will learn to create slides, **handouts** and **notes** like the ones shown here.

Slides

Slides are the part of your presentation that your audience will look at, one at a time. Each slide can have a heading at the top, with words or pictures below it. Most slide shows have about ten slides – more than that may overwhelm your audience.

These are some slides from a presentation about birds.

Words on slides should be easy to read from a distance.

Flying

- The shape of their wings helps birds to fly
  ...unded on top and
  ...s its wings they push

Migration

- Many birds fly from one part of the world to another when the season changes
- Birds migrate to find food and warmer weather

Heading

Birds

Flightless birds

- Penguins
- Ostriches
- Kiwis
- Rheas
- Cassowaries

Pictures make slides look more interesting.

You can show your own drawings on your slides.

Pop Art print

These slides show some of the other things you can do with PowerPoint.

A column chart

Annual quarterly sales

(chart with categories: 1st Qtr, 2nd Qtr, 3rd Qtr, 4th Qtr; legend: mail order, shops, promotions; y-axis 0 to 350)

A table

Timetable of classes

	Monday	Tuesday	Wednesday	Thursday	Fri...
dance	Sam		Sam	Carla	La...
yoga	Carla	Laura		Laura	Rob
step	Laura	Sam	Rob		Carla
gym	Rob		Carla	Rob	Sam

Tim's Tennis Tips

Spacesuits

- Insulate from extreme heat and cold in Space
- Supply oxygen for breathing
- Maintain pressure to keep body fluids liquid

You can include photographs in your presentations.

Slides can even include special effects like moving letters and pictures.

Planning

It is a good idea to plan your presentation on paper before you use the computer.

Decide what you want each slide to show and where you want to include pictures, photos or charts. Then, think of a short heading to describe what is shown on each slide.

Your plan doesn't have to be final as it's easy to make changes to your presentation later.

Presentation plan
1. Presentation title – Birds (with pictures of birds)
2. Bird features
3. Eggs (picture of eggs in a nest)
4. Feathers (list the different types of feathers)
5. Flying (diagram to explain how birds fly)
6. Migration (what is migration and why do some birds migrate?)
7. Flightless birds (list of flightless birds with pictures)
8. Birds I spotted in Florida (column chart)

Notes

Notes are for you to read from while you give your presentation. They are not seen by the audience. Each sheet shows a small picture of a slide with notes to remind you what to say or do while your audience is looking at the slide.

Print your notes in black and white to save coloured ink.

Handouts

Handouts are small, printed versions of your slides. You can give them to people to take away after the presentation.

Handouts can be printed in different ways.

This handout shows lots of slides on one sheet. This is useful if you want to save paper.

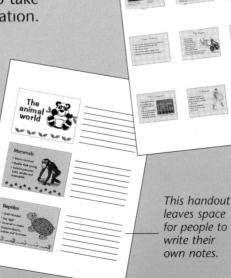

This handout leaves space for people to write their own notes.

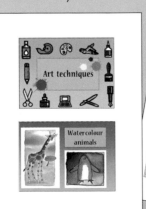

Starting PowerPoint® 2000

Follow these steps to start PowerPoint and open a blank presentation that you can add words, pictures and backgrounds to later on. First you need to find out how to use the **mouse**.

Using the mouse

As you move the mouse, a small arrow, called the **pointer**, moves around the screen. Press and release the left mouse button. This is called **clicking**. Clicking is used to tell the computer to do something. As you work through this book, always use the left mouse button to click. If you are told to **right-click**, press the right mouse button instead.

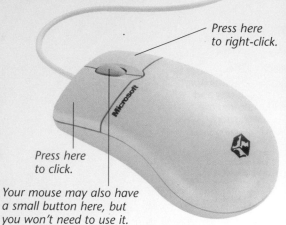

Press here to right-click.

Press here to click.

Your mouse may also have a small button here, but you won't need to use it.

Move the pointer here and click to start.

Click here to begin.

Start

1. Switch your computer on. When you see the Windows® screen, click on *Start* in the bottom left-hand corner.

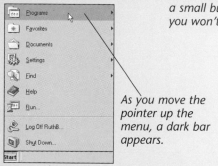

As you move the pointer up the menu, a dark bar appears.

2. A list, called a **menu** appears. Move the pointer up the menu and click on the word *Programs*.

If Microsoft PowerPoint isn't on the menu, turn to page 44.

3. A second menu appears. If *Microsoft PowerPoint* is on the menu, move the pointer over it and click.

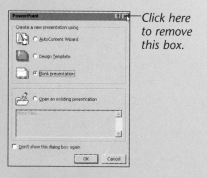

Click here to remove this box.

4. If this box appears, click on the tiny x in the top right-hand corner to remove it. Otherwise, go to step 5.

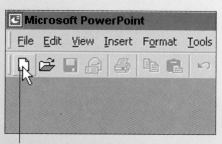

The New tool looks like a sheet of blank paper.

5. Move the pointer to the top left-hand corner of the screen. Now click on the New **tool**.

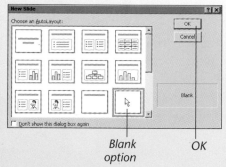

Blank option

OK

6. A New Slide box appears in the middle of the screen. Click on the Blank option. Now click on *OK*.

The PowerPoint window

Your screen now looks like this one. This is the PowerPoint **window**, which is divided into three separate sections called **panes**.

Don't worry if your screen doesn't look exactly like this one as computer screens can be set up to look slightly different.

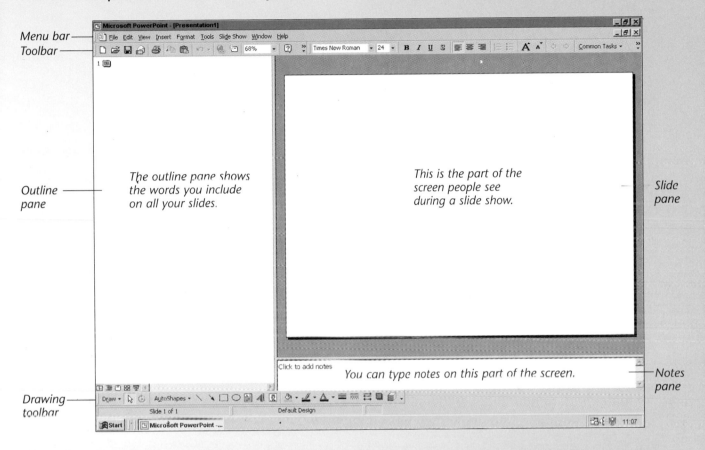

Menu bar

Toolbar

Outline pane

The outline pane shows the words you include on all your slides.

This is the part of the screen people see during a slide show.

Slide pane

Drawing toolbar

You can type notes on this part of the screen.

Notes pane

Tools

Using the tools is often the quickest way to tell your computer to do something. You may not see all the tools shown below because PowerPoint shows only the tools that are used most often. It's easy to find a tool that seems to be missing. Just click on one of the sets of double arrows at the end of the **toolbar** and the missing tools appear. If you can't see the toolbars on your screen, you can turn to page 44 for help.

These are some of the tools you will find out how to use:

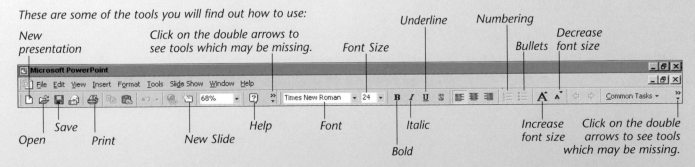

New presentation

Click on the double arrows to see tools which may be missing.

Underline

Numbering

Decrease font size

Font Size

Bullets

Open

Save

Print

Help

New Slide

Font

Italic

Bold

Increase font size

Click on the double arrows to see tools which may be missing.

Creating a presentation

Your first slide is created as soon as you start to type. These steps show you how to make a new slide for each heading in your presentation and to move from one slide to another. You'll also find out about other things that may happen as you type. First, you need to explore the keyboard.

The keyboard

As you start to type, you may find the keyboard confusing. Don't worry – you won't use all the keys. Here are some of the keys you will find useful.

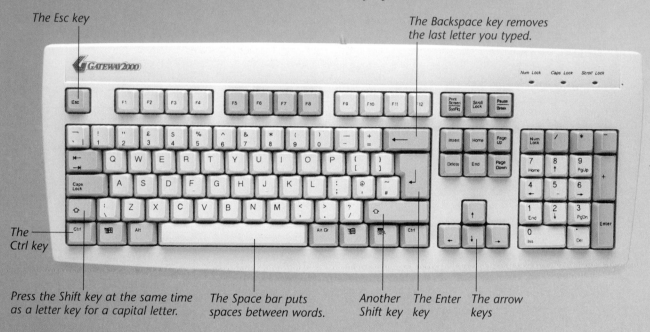

The Esc key

The Backspace key removes the last letter you typed.

The Ctrl key

Press the Shift key at the same time as a letter key for a capital letter.

The Space bar puts spaces between words.

Another Shift key

The Enter key

The arrow keys

Starting to type

The insertion point appears here.

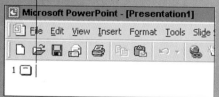

The Slide pane shows what your first slide looks like so far.

1. In the top left-hand corner of the Outline pane, is a tiny, numbered picture of a slide. Click to the right of it to see the **insertion point**.

2. Type the title of your presentation. As you type, the title also appears in the Slide pane. Now press the Enter key on the keyboard.

3. A second slide appears. Type the next slide heading from your plan. Press Enter again and continue typing the rest of your headings.

Getting around

The Slide pane shows one slide at a time, and the Outline pane shows all the words you have typed so far. These steps show you some ways to move from one slide to another.

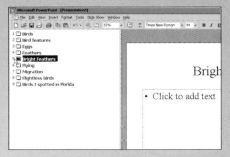

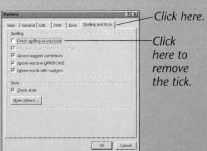

The insertion point moves up or down the Outline pane.

1. Move the pointer over the Outline pane and click on the number of the slide you want to see. That slide now appears in the Slide pane.

2. To see the next slide, press the Ctrl key at the same time as the down arrow. To see the previous slide, press Ctrl and the up arrow key.

Office Assistant

The Office Assistant is a moving character that usually looks like a paper clip. It offers helpful tips, but its advice can be complicated for beginners.

Click here to remove the Office Assistant.

To hide the Office Assistant, right-click on it. A menu pops up. Click on *Hide*. You can find out more about using the Office Assistant on page 45.

Spelling

While you type, red wiggly lines may appear under some words. This is the computer's way of telling you that the word may be misspelled. This is useful, but can be distracting, so follow these steps to remove them. Don't worry about these lines though – they don't appear on the final slide show, or on printed handouts.

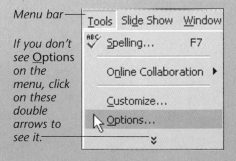

Menu bar

If you don't see Options on the menu, click on these double arrows to see it.

1. To remove the red wiggly lines, click on *Tools* on the Menu bar. A menu appears. Move the pointer down the menu and click on *Options*.

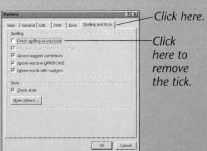

Click here.

Click here to remove the tick.

2. A box appears. Click on *Spelling and Style* near the top of the box. Click on *Check spelling as you type* to remove the tick, then on *OK*.

Light bulb

A small picture of a light bulb may also pop up as you type. You can click on it for advice about your writing style, but it may distract you. Here's how to switch it off.

Click here to remove the tick.

Follow the steps you used to hide the red wiggly lines. This time, click on *Check style* to remove the tick, then click on *OK*.

Saving your work

You now need to **save** what you've done so far. Saving is a way of storing your work on the computer so that you can work on it later. If you switch off your computer without saving, then you will have to start all over again. To save your presentation, first you need to create a **folder** to store it in.

Creating a new folder

Save tool   *Save As box*   *Create New Folder tool*

Menu bar
Toolbar

1. Click on the Save tool, near the left-hand end of the toolbar. The Save As box (see right) appears on the screen.

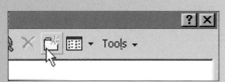

2. Now, click on the Create New Folder tool near the top right-hand corner of the Save As box.

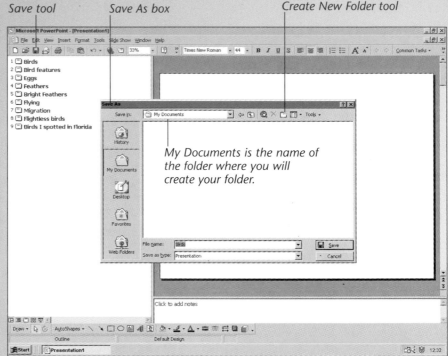

My Documents is the name of the folder where you will create your folder.

Type the name of your folder in this space.   *Click on OK.*

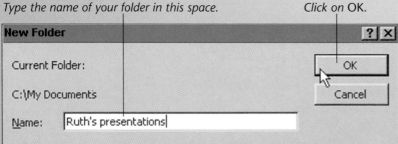

3. The New Folder box appears. The insertion point is flashing inside a long white space, labelled *Name*.

4. Choose a name for your folder that you'll remember easily. Type it into this space, then click on *OK*.

5. The New Folder box vanishes. Your folder's name now appears at the top of the Save As box.

Saving

Now you can save your presentation in the folder you've created. To do this, you need to give it a name, which your computer calls a **file name**. You can use your presentation's title as its file name, or you can give it another name.

You can save as many presentations as you like in one folder. You can also store pictures and other work in it too. If several people are sharing a computer, they can all create their own folders.

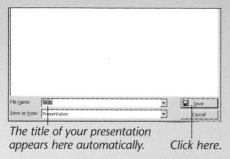

The title of your presentation appears here automatically. *Click here.*

1. To use the title of your presentation as its file name, click on *Save* on the Save As box and go to step 4.

2. To save your presentation with a different file name, click to the right of the title in the *File name* space.

Save tool

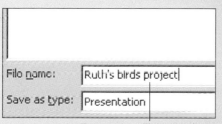

Type a new file name here.

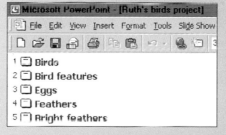

3. Press the Backspace key until the title is removed. Now type a new file name and click on *Save*.

4. The Save As box vanishes and the presentation's file name appears in the top left-hand corner of the screen.

5. Now you've named your presentation, you can save any changes you make by clicking on the Save tool.

More on saving

Every time you save changes to your presentation, the original version is lost and replaced by the new one. To save changes without losing the original version, use *Save As*. This is handy if you want to use the same presentation with small changes for different audiences.

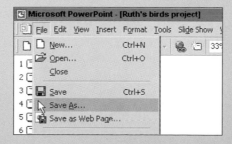

1. To save a new version of your presentation, click on *File*. Now click on *Save As*. The Save As box appears.

New presentation file name.

2. Type a new name in the *File name* space. Click on *Save*. Both versions are now saved in your folder.

Adding words

It's time to start adding words to your slides. The words are the information you want to show on each slide. In PowerPoint these words are called **text**. Normally, your first slide will show your presentation title but no text.

A 'bulleted' list

Below the heading on the Slide pane is a dotted box outline, which contains the words 'Click to add text'. This is a **text box**. The words you type into it appear as a list of points with a small round dot to mark each new point. These dots are called **bullets**.

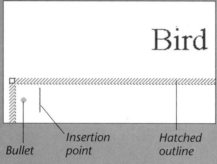

You can find out how to remove bullet points, or change them into numbers on page 27.

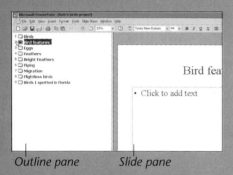

Outline pane　　　*Slide pane*

1. In the Outline pane, click on your second slide so that it appears in the Slide pane. Now click on *Click to add text* in the Slide pane.

Bullet　　*Insertion point*　　*Hatched outline*

2. The words vanish and the outline around the text box changes to a hatched line. The insertion point appears, ready for you to type.

3. As you type, the words appear in the text box on the slide. They also appear under the heading in the Outline pane.

4. To type your next point, press the Enter key on the keyboard. The insertion point and a new bullet appear on the next line.

5. After you've finished this slide, save your work. Now add words to the other slides in your presentation in the same way.

The first word of each point automatically starts with a capital letter, even if you forget to type it.

12

Shrinking letters

As you add bulleted lists to your slides, you may notice the letters shrinking and shifting closer together without you meaning them to. Don't panic – this is just the computer's way of letting you know that you've added too many lines of text. These steps illustrate what happens when letters start shrinking.

Remember to keep saving your work as you go along. A quick way to save is to press Ctrl and S on the keyboard at the same time.

Great Italian food
- Pizza with anchovies and peppers on top
- Macaroni
- Pasta in rich tomato sauce
- Ravioli with beef filling
- Green olives stuffed with pimento
- Salami sausage
- Gorgonzola blue cheese

1. Your words appear on the slides in a size the audience can read easily. At this size, seven lines fit in a text box.

Great Italian food
- Pizza with anchovies and peppers on top
- Macaroni
- Pasta in rich tomato sauce
- Ravioli with beef filling
- Green olives stuffed with pimento
- Salami sausage
- Gorgonzola blue cheese
- Tiramisu coffee dessert with cream

2. With eight or nine lines, the letters shrink and the lines move closer together so they still fit in the text box.

Great Italian food
- Pizza with anchovies and peppers on top
- Macaroni
- Pasta in rich tomato sauce
- Ravioli with beef filling
- Green olives stuffed with pimento
- Salami sausage
- Gorgonzola blue cheese
- Tiramisu coffee dessert with cream
- Cappuccino
- Almond biscuits

3. If you add any more lines, your words spill out of the text box. This is difficult to read from a distance.

Less is best

To avoid shrinking letters, try not to type more than seven lines of text onto a slide. Your presentation will be more effective if you keep sentences short and simple. Fewer words on a slide make it easier for your audience to read. It also leaves more space for pictures.

Keep the text on your slides short and simple.

Great Italian food
- Pizza
- Pasta
- Olives
- Salami
- Gorgonzola
- Tiramisu

Add a big picture to a slide that has only a few words.

Bird features
- Wings
- Feathers
- Beak
- Light, hollow bones

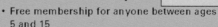

Giants
Junior Sports
- Free membership for anyone between ages 5 and 15
- Soccer, gymnastics, athletics and more
- We take part in local and national competitions

Adding pictures

Once all your words are in place, you can add pictures to your presentation. Follow these steps to add a **Clip Art** picture to your title slide. Don't worry if the picture hides part of the title – you'll find out how to move and change the size of pictures on pages 16-17.

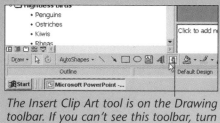

The Insert Clip Art tool is on the Drawing toolbar. If you can't see this toolbar, turn to page 44 for help.

Click on this arrow to see more.

1. Click on the title slide in the Outline pane of the screen, so that the title slide appears in the Slide pane.

2. Click on the Insert Clip Art tool. If a box appears, telling you that the computer needs to add pictures, click on *OK*.

3. The Insert ClipArt box appears. The pictures are sorted into categories. Click on *Animals* to choose it.

4. A selection of pictures appears (see right). Click on a picture you would like to add to your title slide.

5. A menu pops up next to the picture. Click on the Insert Clip tool at the top of the menu.

6. The menu disappears. Now, click on the tiny x in the top corner to remove the Insert ClipArt box.

This is a selection of pictures from the animals category.

Click here to see the choice of categories again.

Click here to close the box.

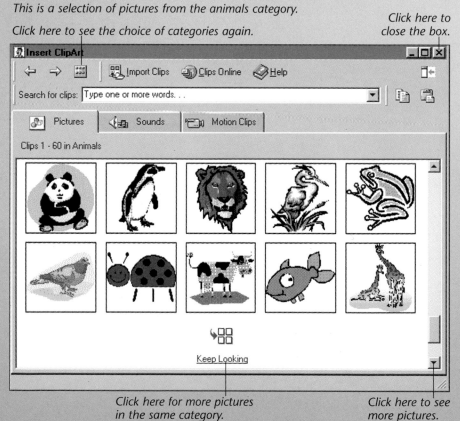

Click here for more pictures in the same category.

Click here to see more pictures.

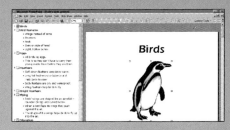

Click here to remove the toolbar.

7. The picture now appears on your slide. If the Picture toolbar also appears, click on the x at the top to remove it.

8. If you don't like the picture after all, press the Delete key on the keyboard. The picture is removed.

9. Choose a new picture and add it to your slide. There are eight tiny squares around it. These are called **handles**.

10. If you're happy with the picture, click away from it so that the handles disappear. Now save your work.

You can't delete a picture unless it has handles around it. To make handles appear around a picture, simply click on it.

You can add lots of pictures to one slide. These slides show some different ways you can use Clip Art pictures.

The picture on a title slide should show what the presentation is about.

Clip Art from a CD-ROM

Sometimes, when you try to insert a Clip Art picture, you may see a message which tells you that it is stored on the disc, or **CD-ROM** that Microsoft® PowerPoint® 2000 came on. It's easy to add these pictures – find the CD-ROM the message tells you the picture is on, and follow these steps.

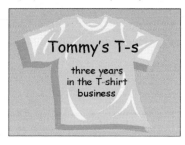

Combine pictures and text to keep your audience interested.

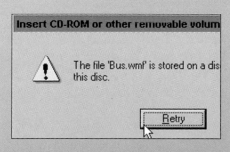

1. If the picture is on the disc, you'll see a message like this one. Place the disc in the CD-ROM drive.

2. Wait until the disc stops whirring. Click on *Retry*. The message vanishes and the picture appears on the slide.

Try to use pictures that might appeal to the age of your audience.

Pictures and text

You can now add pictures to the rest of your presentation. Clip Art pictures automatically appear in the middle of a slide and may hide some of the text. These pages show how easy it is to **resize**, and rearrange pictures and text so that they work together.

Changing a picture's size

To change the size of a picture, you use an action called **clicking and dragging**. This means clicking on a picture and holding the left mouse button down while you move, or drag, the pointer. First, add a picture to your second slide.

1. Click anywhere on the picture. This **selects** it. Eight handles appear around it. Move the pointer over a corner handle.

2. Click and hold the mouse button down. Now, drag the pointer toward the picture to shrink it, or away from it to enlarge it.

3. As you drag, a dotted outline shows you how big the picture will be.

4. Release the mouse button. The picture changes to the size you have chosen.

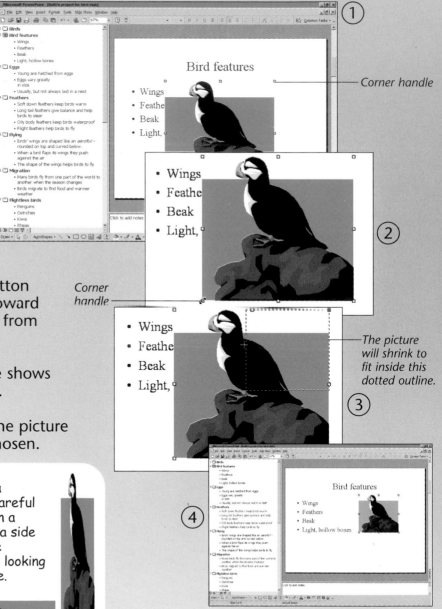

Corner handle

Corner handle

The picture will shrink to fit inside this dotted outline.

The picture now changes to its new size.

When you change a picture's size, be careful to click and drag on a corner handle, not a side one. Otherwise the picture may end up looking squashed like these.

Moving a picture

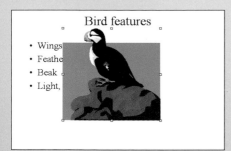

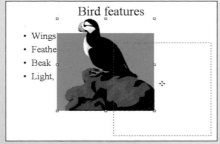

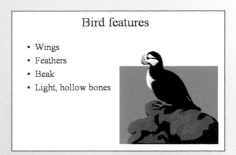

1. Move the pointer over any part of the picture and click to select it. Hold the mouse button down.

2. Drag the pointer to where you want to move the picture. A dotted outline shows where it will be.

3. Release the mouse button. The picture moves to its new position on the slide. Now save what you've done.

Text boxes

Text boxes and headings have handles too. You can move and resize them in the same way as pictures. Simply click and drag.

1. Click on a word. Eight handles and a hatched outline appear around the text box.

2. Click and drag on any handle around the text box to change its size or shape.

3. To move a text box, click on its outline and drag it to a new position.

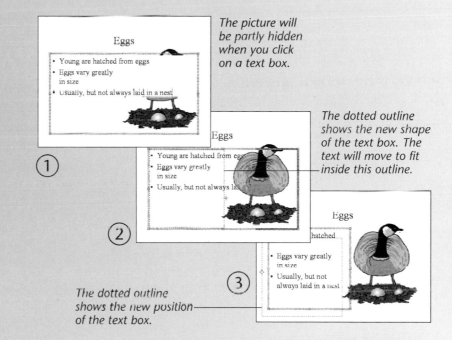

The picture will be partly hidden when you click on a text box.

The dotted outline shows the new shape of the text box. The text will move to fit inside this outline.

The dotted outline shows the new position of the text box.

Don't:

Add pictures that hide the writing or that don't go with it. Badly-chosen pictures might confuse people who are watching your presentation.

The pictures on this slide cover the writing and don't show what the slide is about.

Do:

Use bright pictures. Slides without much writing on them look much more interesting if you use pictures to illustrate the text.

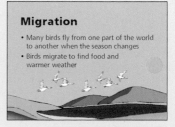

You'll learn how to change the style of the lettering on your slides on pages 26-27.

Adding your own pictures

As well as Clip Art, you can include your own pictures in your presentations. These could be pictures you have created using a drawing program, such as Microsoft® Paint, or drawings and photos that you've scanned. Make sure that you save all your pictures in the folder you created earlier in My Documents so that you can find them easily.

Here are some of the different kinds of pictures you could add to your slides.

These pictures were created on a computer using Microsoft® Paint.

Photos and drawings that have been scanned into a computer can also be included on your slides.

A new category

To add your own pictures to a presentation, you will bring them from your folder into PowerPoint. This is called **importing**. To import your pictures, you need to create your own picture category in the Insert ClipArt box.

1. Click on the Insert Clip Art tool at the bottom of the screen. In the Insert ClipArt box, click on *New Category*.

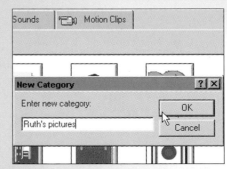

2. The New Category box pops up. Click on the white space and type a name for your category. Click on *OK*.

Categories are arranged alphabetically.

3. Your new picture category now appears with the other Clip Art categories. Move the pointer over it and click.

Click here to import your pictures.

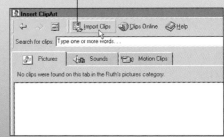

4. You'll see a white space and a message telling you that no clips were found. Click on *Import Clips*.

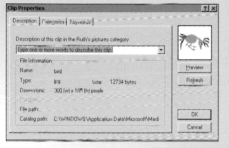

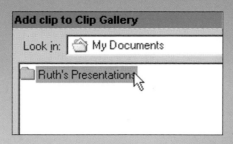

5. A box pops up. Click on the tiny arrow near the top of the box. A list appears. Now click on *My Documents.*

6. My Documents appears at the top of the box with your folder in the space below it. Click twice on your folder.

7. A list of all the pictures in your folder appears. Click on the name of the picture you want to use, then on *Import.*

8. The Clip Properties box appears. Press the Backspace key to remove the words in the Description space.

9. Type the name of your picture into the Description space of the Clip Properties box and click on *OK.*

10. The picture appears in the Insert ClipArt box. Add the rest of your pictures to your category in the same way.

11. Now add a picture from your new category to a slide and move or resize it in the same way as normal Clip Art.

It's a good idea to create a new picture category for each new presentation.

The pictures in your category can be added to any presentation.

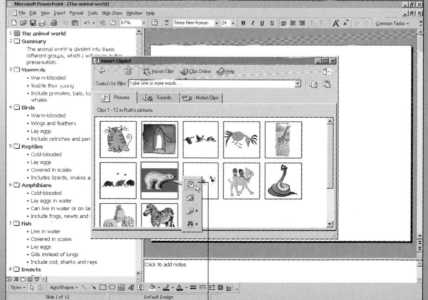

Click here to add your picture to this slide.

Adding shapes

Another way to make a presentation look brighter is to decorate your slides with coloured shapes. To do this you'll need to use tools on the Drawing toolbar. If you can't see the toolbar, turn to page 44 for help.

Click here if you can't see Stars and Banners.

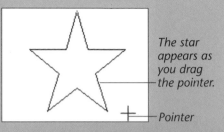

The star appears as you drag the pointer.

Pointer

1. Click on a slide you want to add shapes to. Click on *Autoshapes*. A menu pops up. Click on *Stars and Banners*, then on a star shape.

2. Move the pointer over the Slide pane. Click and drag the pointer to make the star appear on the slide in the size you want.

3. Release the mouse button. The star appears on your slide. It has eight handles around it, and may be filled with a colour.

Your menu may not show the same colours as this one.

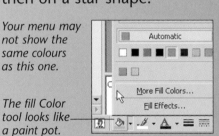

The fill Color tool looks like a paint pot.

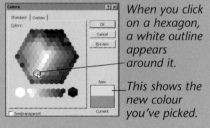

When you click on a hexagon, a white outline appears around it.

This shows the new colour you've picked.

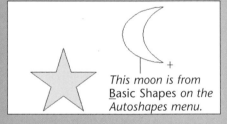

This moon is from Basic Shapes on the Autoshapes menu.

4. To change the colour, click on the arrow next to the Fill Color tool. A menu appears with a selection of colours. Click on *More Fill Colors*.

5. The Colors box pops up. Pick any coloured hexagon and click on it, then on *OK*. The Colors box vanishes and the star changes colour.

6. Now you can draw and colour some other shapes in the same way, using different shapes from the Autoshapes menu.

These title slides have been decorated with shapes from the Autoshapes menus.

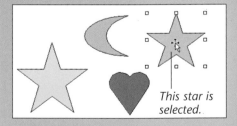

This star is selected.

7. Click on a shape to select it. You can delete, move or resize any selected shape in the same way as you did with pictures.

Adding new text boxes

You can have more than one text box on a slide. This means that you can add labels to your pictures and even speech bubbles. These steps show you how to add a plain text box and a speech bubble to a slide.

1. To create a plain text box, click on the Text Box tool, on the Drawing toolbar, near the bottom left-hand corner of the screen.

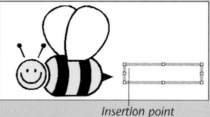

Insertion point

2. Click and drag on a blank part of the slide to create a text box. Release the mouse button, and an insertion point appears inside the box.

These slides show how you can use extra text boxes and speech bubbles.

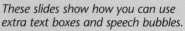

Extra text boxes can be used to label your pictures.

3. Type some words. The box expands downward as you type. You can resize or move this text box in the same way as a normal text box.

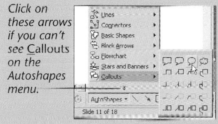

Click on these arrows if you can't see Callouts on the Autoshapes menu.

4. To create a speech bubble, click on *Autoshapes*, then on *Callouts*. Click on one of the shapes. Now, click and drag on the slide to draw it.

These arrows were added from the Autoshapes menu.

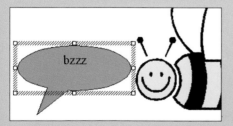

5. An insertion point flashes in the middle of the speech bubble. Type some text, then use the Fill Color tool to make the bubble white.

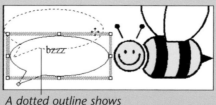

A dotted outline shows the bubble's new position.

6. Click within the speech bubble, but away from the text. Hold the mouse button down and drag the pointer to move the bubble.

Yellow handle *A dotted outline shows where the point will be.*

7. To move the point of the speech bubble to the right place, click on the yellow handle and drag it to where you want. Now save.

Adding a table

You may want to include a timetable or statistics in your presentation. A table is an effective way to display this kind of information so that it is easy for your audience to understand at a glance. These steps show how to add a table to a slide with a heading on it.

These two yellow slides both show the same number information. The table is much clearer.

Try not to include too much information on a table – keep it simple.

Medals won this season

Medal	Ruth	Ben	Rebecca	Isaac
Gold	3	1	2	1
Silver	2	1	3	4
Bronze	1	2	1	1

This table has 5 columns and 4 rows. The first column and the top row show headings.

Medals won this season

- Ruth got the most gold medals. She won 3 gold, 2 silver and 1 bronze
- Ben, our new member, got 1 gold, 1 silver and 2 bronze medals
- Rebecca got 6 medals in total. She won 2 gold medals, 3 silver and 1 bronze
- Isaac, last year's champion, won a gold medal, a bronze and 4 silver medals

Some space travel firsts

Year	First...
1957	dog in space – Laika
1961	man in space – Yuri Gagarin
1963	woman in space – Valentina Tereshkova
1965	space walk – Alexei Leonov
1966	lunar landing – Luna 9
1969	moonwalk – Neil Armstrong

It's a good idea to plan your table on paper first, so that you know how many columns and rows you want it to have.

1. Click on the slide you want to add a table to. Move the pointer to the Menu bar and click on *Format*. Now click on *Slide Layout*.

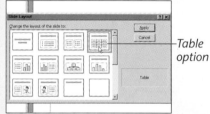

—Table option

2. The Slide Layout box pops up. To add a table, click on the Table option in the top right-hand corner of the box. Now click on *Apply*.

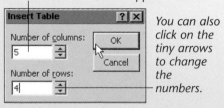

Double-click on this picture.

The number of columns appears here.

You can also click on the tiny arrows to change the numbers.

3. A tiny picture of a table appears on the slide. Move the pointer over it and click twice, quickly. This is called **double-clicking.**

4. The Insert Table box pops up. Type the number of vertical columns you want. Press the Tab key, then type the number of horizontal rows.

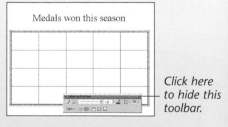

Click here to hide this toolbar.

5. Click on *OK*. A table appears on your slide. If the Tables and Borders toolbar appears, click on the x in the right-hand corner to hide it.

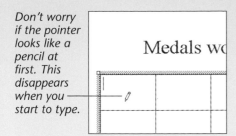

Don't worry if the pointer looks like a pencil at first. This disappears when you start to type.

Medals wc

The pointer changes shape when it is over a line.

n	Rebecca	Isaac
	2	1

6. An insertion point is in the first box. Type a column heading, then click on the next box to type into it. Fill in each box in the table.

7. To change the width of a column to fit longer words, click on a vertical line and drag the pointer away from the word. Now save.

Colouring a table

Now that you have created your table, you can use the Fill Color tool near the bottom of the screen, to add colour to it. This makes the information stand out.

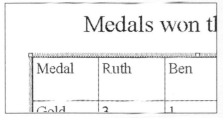

Medals won tl

Medal	Ruth	Ben
Gold	3	1

this season

	Rebecca	Isaac
	2	1
	3	4
	1	1

1. To fill a table with a colour, click on the outline around it. The outline changes from a hatched line, to a shaded line.

2. Now, click on the arrow next to the Fill Color tool. Click on *More Fill Colors*. The Colors box appears. Click on a colour, then on *OK*.

Medals won this season

Medal	Ruth	Ben	Rebecca	Isaac
Gold	3	1	2	1
Silver	2	1	3	4

Medals won this season

Medal	Ruth	Ben	Rebecca	Isaac
Gold	3	1	2	1
Silver	2	1	3	4

3. To change the colour of a whole row, click on the first box and drag the pointer to the end of the row. A dark area appears over the row.

4. Use the Fill Color tool as before. The row changes colour. Now save. You can change the colour of columns in the same way.

It's best not to use very dark colours, as they may make the text difficult to read.

Timetable of classes

	Monday	Tuesday	Wednesday	Thursday	Friday
dance	Sam		Sam	Carla	Laura
yoga	Carla	Laura		Laura	Rob
step	Laura	Sam	Rob		Carla
gym	Rob		Carla	Rob	Sam

Our star signs

Name	Birthday	Star sign
Karen	October 10th	Libra
Max	April 1st	Aries
Jim	August 20th	Leo
Louis	June 2nd	Gemini
Nina	January 30th	Aquarius

Our timetable of activities

Day	Morning	Afternoon
Monday	Arrive in Rome	Piazza Navona
Tuesday	The Forum	Circus Maximus
Wednesday	National museum	The Colosseum
Thursday	The Vatican	Sistine Chapel
Friday	Luna park	Return home

You can find out how to add coloured or textured backgrounds to your slides on pages 28-29.

Adding a column chart

A column chart is a brighter, more interesting way to show the same information as a number table. It's easy to create a chart in PowerPoint – all you do is type your information into a table called a **datasheet**, and it instantly appears on the slide as a column chart.

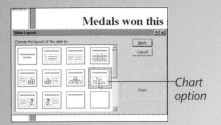

Chart option

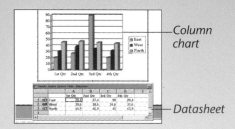

Column chart

Datasheet

Try not to include too much data on one slide. Your audience probably won't have very long to read it.

1. Open a slide you want to add a chart to. Click on *Format*, then on *Slide Layout*. A box appears. Click on the Chart option, then on *Apply*.

2. A picture of a chart appears. Double-click on it. A sample column chart and a datasheet appear. Both show the same data differently.

The pointer changes to a cross.

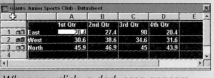

When you click, a dark area appears over the datasheet.

3. To remove the sample data, click on the grey box in the top left-hand corner of the datasheet. Press Delete on the keyboard.

When you click on a white box, a dark outline appears around it.

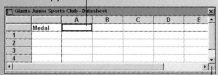

Click on these arrows for more squares.

4. The numbers are cleared. Click on the first black box. The datasheet turns white. Type a column heading. Click on the next white box.

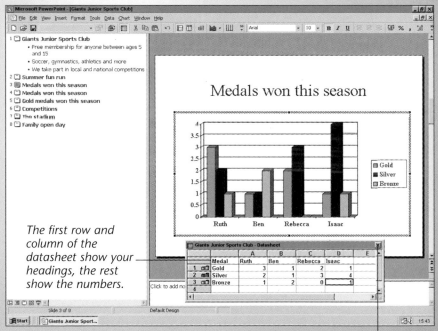

The first row and column of the datasheet show your headings, the rest show the numbers.

To close the datasheet, click on the x in the top right-hand corner.

5. Type the rest of your headings and numbers. The chart appears above the datasheet as you type. Now, close the datasheet.

6. The chart stays on the slide with eight handles around it. Click on a corner of the slide so that the handles disappear. Save.

Changing a column chart

Once you've created a chart there are several ways you can change its appearance. You may want to change the statistics or add more data. It's also easy to change the colours. Follow these steps to find out how it's done.

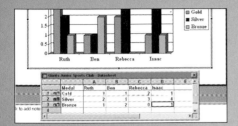

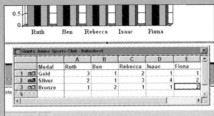

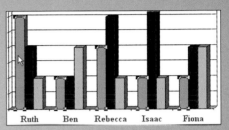

1. To change any of the numbers, or to add new numbers, double-click on the chart so that the datasheet appears again.

2. If it doesn't appear, click on *View* on the Menu bar, then on *Datasheet*. To type your changes, click on a box in the datasheet. Press Enter.

3. To change the colours, click on a column. Make sure four handles appear around each column of the same colour. Double-click.

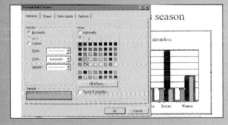

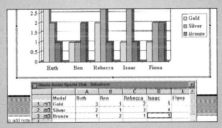

4. The Format Data Series box pops up. Click on a coloured square, then on *OK*. The set of columns changes to that colour.

5. Once you're pleased with the changes you've made to your chart, click on the datasheet and close it. Now save your presentation.

You can move a chart on your slide by clicking and dragging on it.

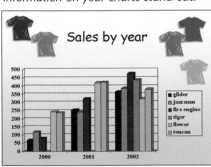

Use strong colours to make the information on your charts stand out.

Use pictures to illustrate your charts.

On pages 28-29 you'll find out how to add backgrounds to your slides.

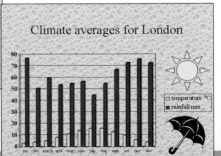

Changing lettering and bullets

The words you add to your slides automatically appear in plain lettering, but it's easy to change the way they look by using the tools along the top of the screen. If you can't see these tools, turn to page 44.

Selecting text

Before you can change the appearance of your text, you need to select it. You can click and drag to select a single word or a group of words. It's also easy to select a whole text box so that any changes you make affect everything inside the box at the same time.

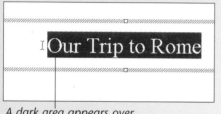

A dark area appears over the selected words.

1. To select a word, or group of words, click to the left of the text and drag the pointer to the end.

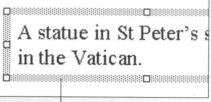

A shaded outline shows that this text box is selected.

2. To select a whole text box, press and hold the Shift key on the keyboard as you click on a word in the box.

All the text boxes on this slide are selected.

3. To select several text boxes at once, press and hold the Shift key and click on a word in each box.

Fun lettering

There are lots of lettering styles, called **fonts**, to choose from. Changing the font on your slides is an easy way to make the lettering suit the subject of the presentation.

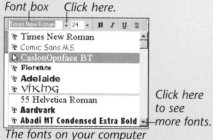

Font box   *Click here.*

Click here to see more fonts.

The fonts on your computer may be different from these.

1. Select the text you want to change. Click on the arrow next to the Font box. A list of fonts appears.

The name of the font you've chosen appears here.

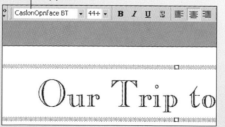

2. Click on the name of the font you want to use. The selected text changes to that style of lettering. Now save.

The list of fonts should show what each of them looks like. If the fonts on your list all seem to look the same, turn to page 44.

Bigger and smaller

Increase Font Size tool

Decrease Font Size tool

1. To make selected text bigger, click on the Increase Font Size tool. Keep clicking until the text is the right size.

2. Click on the Decrease Font Size tool if you want to make selected lettering go down in size.

Lettering styles

Bold tool   Italic tool

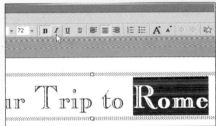

1. To make selected text look **thicker**, click on the Bold tool. Click on the Italic tool to make the text *slant*.

2. The tools are like on/off switches. Click on the Italic tool again to make selected letters straight again.

Bullets and numbers

Bullets tool

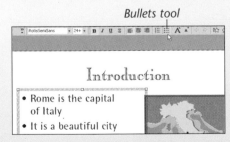

Numbering tool

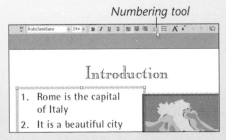

1. To remove bullets from a selected text box, click on the Bullets tool. Click on the tool again to add them.

2. To change a bulleted list in a selected text box into a numbered list, click on the Numbering tool.

These slides show some different effects you can achieve by changing the appearance of the lettering.

★ A guide to living in Space by Paul Mazonas ★

These space-age fonts suit the subject of this presentation.

Bold or italic lettering makes headings and other words stand out.

Larger lettering makes the text on the slide clear and easy to read.

Too many fancy fonts make a slide look messy and difficult to read.

Backgrounds

Your presentation is almost complete, but the slides may look rather bare. Adding backgrounds to your slides is a finishing touch that will brighten them up. First it's a good idea to change the **view** of the screen so that you can see all the slides at once and decide which colours will work best.

Coloured backgrounds

Slide Sorter View tool

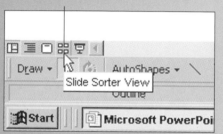

1. To change your screen, click on the Slide Sorter View tool in the bottom left-hand corner of the screen.

This screen is in Slide Sorter View.

2. Click on the first slide. Click on *Format* on the Menu bar. A menu appears. Click on *Background*.

Click on this arrow, then on More Colors to see a choice of colours.

3. The Background box pops up. Click on the down arrow so that a menu appears. Now click on *More Colors*.

If you don't see this selection of colours, click on Standard.

4. A selection of colours appears. Pick one, then click on *OK*. The Background box appears again.

5. To add the colour to the slide you clicked on, click on *Apply*. Add colours to all of your slides in the same way.

You can add the same background to all your slides at once, by clicking on *Apply to All* in step 5.

Adding different coloured backgrounds brings variety to slides that otherwise look quite similar.

Caricatures

Watercolour animals

Pastel polar bear

Computer art

Shaded backgrounds

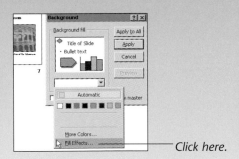

Click here.

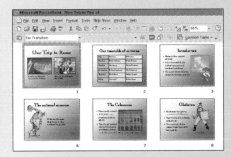

Click here to change the colours.

The sample shows the look of the background.

1. Click on a slide. Click on *Format*, then on *Background*. Click on the down arrow, then on *Fill Effects*.

2. The Fill Effects box pops up. Click on *Two colors*. Click on the down arrow next to each colour to change it.

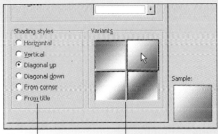

Shading styles   *Variants*

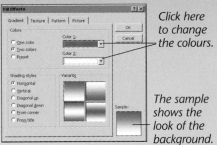

3. To change the direction of shading, click on a shading style and one of the four variants. Click on *OK*.

4. To add the shaded background you've chosen, click on *Apply* or *Apply to All*. Now save your presentation.

Textured backgrounds

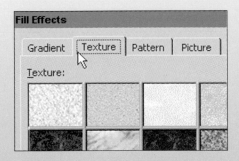

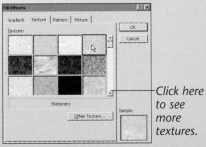

Click here to see more textures.

1. Open the Fill Effects box, as above (see step 1). Now click on *Texture* at the top of the box.

2. Click on a texture you like, then on *OK*. Click on *Apply* or *Apply to All*. Save your changes.

Shaded and textured backgrounds look great, but they shouldn't distract from what is on the slide.

This background complements the photographs on this slide.

This shaded background makes the slide look eye-catching and dramatic.

Darker textures work better on slides without too much text on them.

You can choose a textured background to suit the subject of your presentation.

Adding and sorting slides

Once you can see all of your slides together, you may decide that you want to add an extra one or change the order of the presentation. This is really simple to do in Slide Sorter View.

Slide Sorter View tool

1. To change the screen to Slide Sorter view, click on the Slide Sorter View tool in the bottom left-hand corner.

New Slide tool

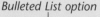
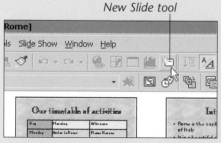

2. To add a new slide, click on your last slide, then click on the New Slide tool near the top of the screen.

Bulleted List option

3. The New Slide box pops up. If the Bulleted List option doesn't have a box around it, click on it. Click on *OK*.

The new slide appears here.

4. The new slide appears after your last slide. To move it, click on it and hold the mouse button down.

The new slide will move to this position.

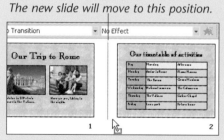

5. Now drag the pointer to where you want to move the slide. A vertical line shows its new position.

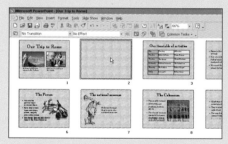

6. Release the mouse button. The slide now appears in its new place. You can move other slides in the same way.

Normal View tool

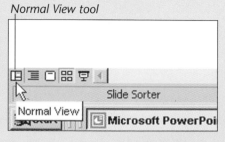

7. To see the new slide in Normal View, double-click on it, or click on the Normal View tool.

8. The slide is now ready for you to add text, pictures and numbers. When you're happy with it, save it.

To delete a slide, click on it in Slide Sorter View, then press the Delete key on the keyboard.

Changing Clip Art colours

Changing the colours of Clip Art pictures will brighten up your slides and allow you to match pictures to the colours of your charts, tables or backgrounds, giving your presentation a more personal touch.

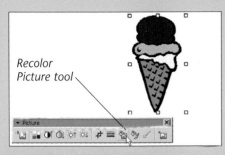

Recolor Picture tool

1. Click on a picture. If the Picture toolbar appears, click on the Recolor Picture tool and go to step 3. If not, right-click on the picture.

2. A menu appears. Move the pointer down the menu to *Show Picture Toolbar* and click. Now click on the Recolor Picture tool.

Click here.

3. The Recolor Picture box appears. Click on an arrow beside a colour you want to change. Some colours appear. Click on *More Colors*.

If you can't see this, click on Standard.

4. A selection of colours appears. Click on a colour you like, then click on *OK*. The new colour replaces the one you selected.

Preview

5. Change the rest of the colours in the same way. When you're pleased with the colours shown in the preview, click on *OK*.

6. The Recolor Picture box vanishes. The colours of the Clip Art picture on your slide are changed. Click away from the picture and save.

You can make several versions of a Clip Art picture by using different colours.

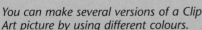

The colours of this helmet have been changed to match the map.

The Recolor Picture tool only works on Clip Art pictures.

Special effects

If you want to bring your slide show to life, try adding some special effects. The way one slide changes into the next is called a **transition**, and you can make words and pictures move using **animation**. Special effects are difficult to show here, but follow these steps to see how they look on-screen. Once you've tried the effects on these pages, there are lots more to try out.

Transition effects

These steps show you how to make a slide drop down over the previous one. You can also include a sound effect.

Sound effects will only work if your computer has speakers.

1. In Normal View, click on your first slide. Click on *Slide Show* on the Menu bar, then on *Slide Transition*.

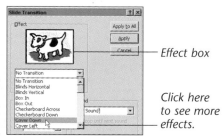

Effect box

Click here to see more effects.

2. The Slide Transition box appears. Click on the down arrow next to *No Transition* and click on *Cover Down*.

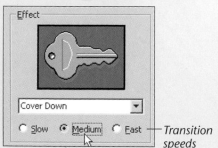

3. The dog picture in the effect box changes to a key to show how the effect looks. Click on the *Medium* speed.

Transition speeds

Click here to see more sound effects.

4. Click on the down arrow below *Sound*. A list of sound effects drops down. Click on *Camera* to select it.

If you want to add the same effect to all your slides, click here.

5. To add these effects to the slide, click on *Apply*. Click on the next slide to add transition effects to it as well.

Animating words and pictures

Follow these steps to make your presentation title fly onto the slide letter-by-letter and to make a picture zoom into place from the middle of the slide.

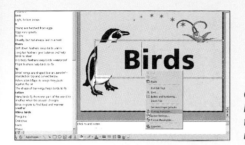

Click here to see more.

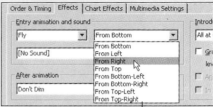

Different animation effects have different options here.

1. With the screen in Normal View, click on your first slide. Right-click on the title. A menu appears. Click on *Custom Animation*.

2. A box appears. Click on the down arrow below *Entry animation and sound*. A list of animation effects drops down. Click on *Fly*.

3. Now click on the next down arrow to the right. A list drops down. It shows different directions to pick. Click on *From Right*.

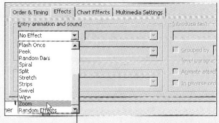

Click here to find Zoom on the menu.

4. To make the title appear a letter at a time, click on the down arrow below *Introduce text*. Click on *By Letter*, then on *OK*. The box vanishes.

5. Right-click on the picture you want to animate. Click on *Custom Animation* again. Click on the down arrow next to *No Effect*.

6. A menu of effects drops down. Click on the down arrow at the bottom of the menu until you can see *Zoom*, then click on it.

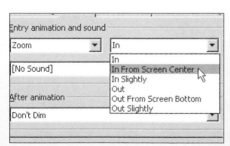

Preview slide

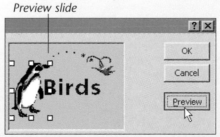

7. Click on the down arrow to the right to see a list of directions for the picture to zoom from. Click on *In From Screen Center*.

8. Click on *Preview*. The preview slide shows how the effects look and sound. Click on *OK* to add the effects to the slide, then save.

To watch some sample slide shows to see special effects in action go to **www.usborne-quicklinks.com** type the keyword "powerpoint" and follow the instructions.

Printing handouts and notes

If you have a printer, you can print small versions of your slides for your own reference, or to give to your audience as handouts. You can also print notes for you to read while you give your presentation.

Before you start

Make sure that the printer is connected to the system unit, then carefully plug it into the mains supply. Switch the power button on and check that there's plenty of paper in the paper tray.

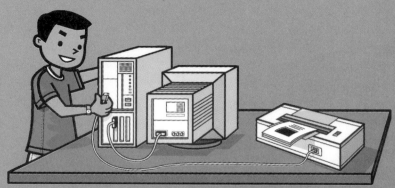

Printing handouts

When you print handouts, you can choose how many slides you want to fit on each piece of paper. Handouts can show between two and nine slides on each each page, depending on how big you want the slides to be.

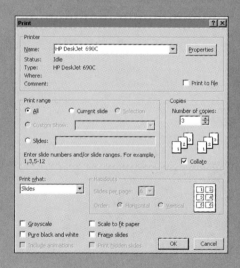

This is the Print box. Yours may not look exactly the same as this one.

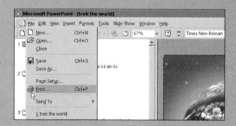

1. Click on *File* in the top left-hand corner of the screen. A menu appears. Click on *Print*.

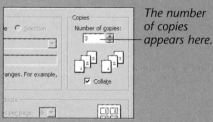

The number of copies appears here.

2. The Print box appears (see right). Now type the number of copies you want to print onto paper.

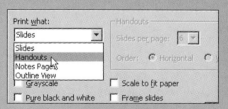

3. To print handouts, click on the down arrow beside *Print what*, then click on *Handouts* on the list.

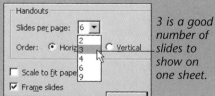

3 is a good number of slides to show on one sheet.

4. Click on the arrow next to *Slides per page* and click on the number of slides you want to print on each page.

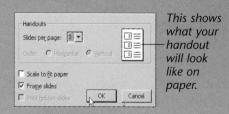

This shows what your handout will look like on paper.

5. Move the pointer to *OK* (or *Print*, depending on the printer) and click to print your handouts.

Printed notes

Some people write notes to remind them what to say or do while they give a presentation. In PowerPoint® 2000, you can create notes on your computer, then print them out. Notes sheets show a small picture of a slide with notes below it.

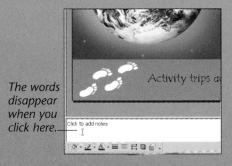

The words disappear when you click here.

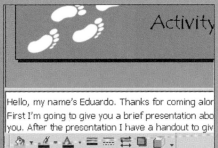

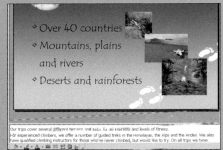

1. In Normal View, click on your first slide. Click on the words 'Click to add notes' below the slide.

2. The insertion point appears. Type any notes that you'll need to refer to while your audience sees the slide.

3. Click on the next slide and type the rest of your notes in the same way. Save your changes before printing.

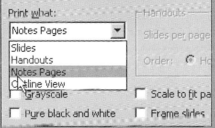

A tick appears here when you click on Grayscale.

4. To print your notes, click on *File*, then *Print* to open the Print box. Type the number of copies you want.

5. Click on the arrow next to *Print what*. A list appears. Move the pointer down the list and click on *Notes Pages*.

6. To print in black and white and avoid wasting coloured ink, click on *Grayscale*. Now click on *OK* to print.

These handouts show some of the different ways you can print them.

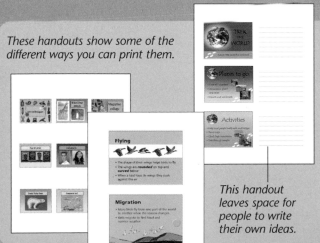

This notes sheet is printed in grayscale.

This handout leaves space for people to write their own ideas.

Make sure there aren't any spelling mistakes on your slides before you print handouts or notes.

Show time

Now it's time to put on your presentation. Whether you want to show your presentation on a computer monitor, or project it onto a large screen, these pages show you how easy it is to set up your show and put it on.

Running the show on a monitor

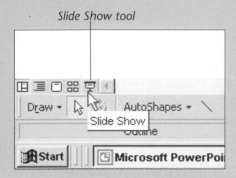

Slide Show tool

1. Click on your title slide, then click on the Slide Show tool in the bottom left-hand corner of the screen. The screen may go black briefly.

2. Your title slide fills the screen. If you've animated any of the objects on the slide, you'll need to click for each one to appear.

3. Click again to see the next slide. At the end of the show, the screen goes dark. Click to to see the title slide again in Normal View.

An automatic show

A slide show can be set up to run while you're not there. Each slide is shown for a few seconds before the next one appears. This is useful if your audience is not used to using computers. The show keeps running until you press Esc on the keyboard.

A dot appears when you click here.

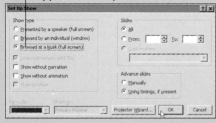

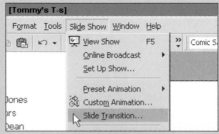

Type a number here. Ten seconds is usually long enough for people to read a slide.

1. Click on a slide, then on *Slide Show* on the Menu bar. Click on *Set Up Show*. A box appears. Click on *Browsed at a kiosk*. Now click on *OK*.

2. Click on *Slide Show* on the Menu bar again. This time, click on *Slide Transition*. The Slide Transition box pops up in the middle of the screen.

3. Type the number of seconds each slide will be shown for. Click on *Apply to All* and save. To run the show, click on the Slide Show tool.

Using a projector with a laptop

If you want to show your presentation on a large screen, you'll need to use a projector. Many people use laptop computers to create and show their presentations, because they are portable and can be taken anywhere. First, connect the projector to the computer. Then plug it into the power supply and switch it on.

You can also attach a projector to a PC, but your computer monitor may not work at the same time as the projector.

You may need to adjust the focus so that the picture is clear.

Cable from the laptop to the projector.

The image on the computer screen is also projected onto the large screen. If it isn't, turn to page 15 for help.

Presentation tips

1. It's a good idea to have a final check through your presentation to make sure that there aren't any mistakes in it.

2. Always make sure that all the equipment is set up and working properly, before your audience arrives.

3. Set up your computer in front of you and stand slightly to one side of the large screen. You'll keep your audience's attention better if you make eye contact with them.

4. Don't give out your handouts until after your presentation as your audience may read them instead of listening to you.

5. Speak slowly and clearly. Try to remember what you want to say so that you don't have to check your notes too often.

6. You can run the show in the same way as on a monitor. If you want to point to a detail on a slide, use the mouse to move the pointer around the screen.

Switching off

It's important to switch off your computer properly, otherwise you may find that it doesn't work very well when you switch it on again. You can avoid problems later, by following the steps on this page.

Closing PowerPoint

Before you close Microsoft® PowerPoint® 2000, you need to save and close your presentation. See pages 10-11 if you can't remember how to save.

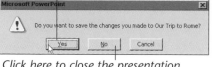

Click here to save any changes you've made.

Click here to close the presentation without saving the changes.

Close

1. To close a presentation, Move the pointer over the lower x in the top right-hand corner of the screen. Click the left mouse button.

2. If this message appears, you've made changes since you saved. To save, click on *Yes* and turn to pages 10-11. Otherwise, click on *No*.

3. To close PowerPoint, click on the cross in the top right-hand corner of the screen. PowerPoint vanishes and the Windows® screen appears.

Shutting down

In computer jargon, switching off is called **shutting down**. These steps show you how it's done.

Click on Shut down so that a dot appears in the circle next to it.

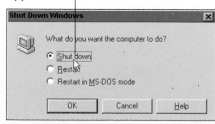

Power buttons

1. Click on Start in the bottom left-hand corner of the screen. A menu appears. Click on *Shut Down*. The menu disappears.

2. A box like this one pops up. Click on *Shut down*, then on *OK*. Wait while the screen changes and the computer prepares to shut itself down.

3. The computer may switch itself off. If not, wait until it tells you that it's ready, then press the power buttons on the system unit and monitor.

Finding a saved presentation

When you save and close a presentation, it disappears from the screen. You need to know how to find it again. These steps show you how to find your work without too much trouble.

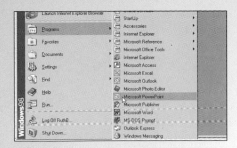

1. If you need to open PowerPoint, click on *Start*. Click on *Programs*, then on *Microsoft PowerPoint*. Otherwise, go to step 4.

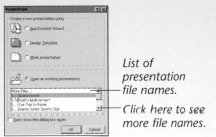

List of presentation file names.

Click here to see more file names.

2. A box appears. Click on *Open an existing presentation*. If your presentation file name appears on the list, click on it, then on *OK* to open it.

Click here.

3. If the file name of the presentation you want to open doesn't appear on the list, click on *More Files*. Now click on *OK* and go to step 5.

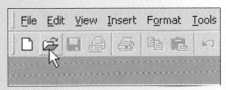

4. If you want to open a presentation and PowerPoint is already open, click on the Open tool near the top left-hand corner of the screen.

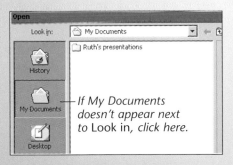

If My Documents doesn't appear next to Look in, *click here.*

5. The Open box appears. When My Documents is next to *Look in*, your folder will be in the box below. Click on your folder, then on *Open*.

The Open box

This arrow appears when there are lots of presentations. Click on it to see more.

You may see the first slide of your presentation in this area.

6. When your folder name is beside *Look in*, the names of your presentations appear in the box below. Find the one you want to open.

7. Click on the name of the presentation you want to open. The first slide may appear to the right. Now click on *Open* to open it.

What do I need?

This book shows you how to use Microsoft® PowerPoint® 2000 on a personal computer or PC. A PC consists of several pieces of equipment, known in computer jargon as **hardware**. You'll also need **software**. Software is the name for computer programs, which give your computer instructions.

Hardware

This picture shows the hardware you will need. All PCs look slightly different, so don't worry if yours doesn't look exactly like this one.

Monitor

This is a printer. If you want to print handouts or notes onto paper, you'll need one of these.

*The **system unit** contains parts that help your computer work. These include the **hard disk drive**, where your computer stores information.*

The CD-ROM drive is used to load software.

Mouse

Keyboard

Software

Software usually comes on a disc, called a CD-ROM, that looks like a music CD. You use the disc to install the software onto your computer. Microsoft® PowerPoint® 2000 is a program that comes as a part of some editions of Microsoft® Office 2000. You'll also need a Microsoft® Windows® 95, 98, 2000 or ME operating system, which is a kind of software that enables other software to work. Find out how to install PowerPoint on pages 42-43.

Projector

If you want to project your slides onto a large screen, you'll need a projector. Page 37 shows you how to use one.

Plugging in

Make sure that the keyboard, monitor and mouse are all properly connected to the system unit. Only push plugs into sockets of the same shape, and make sure that you don't damage the tiny pins that are on some plugs. Don't plug the system unit and monitor in, or switch them on, until everything else is connected.

The back of your computer will look similar to this, but may not look exactly the same.

Cable from the system unit to the mouse

Cable to the keyboard

Cable from the monitor to the power supply

Cable from the system unit to the power supply

Cable to the printer

A cable links the system unit and the monitor

If there are screws on a plug, make sure that you tighten them.

You'll see extra sockets on the back of your computer. These can be used for extra parts, such as speakers.

Switching on

Power buttons

1. Press the power button on the system unit. If there is a button on the monitor, press that too.

2. Wait for a few moments. The computer is ready to use when you see a Windows® screen like the one above.

Although a computer has an on/off button, you shouldn't just switch it off when you've finished using it. Page 38 shows you the proper way to switch off your computer.

Installing PowerPoint® 2000

Microsoft® PowerPoint® 2000 comes as part of Microsoft® Office 2000. When you buy it, you are given a disc, called a CD-ROM. If PowerPoint isn't on your computer yet, you'll need to **install**, or load, it from the CD-ROM.

On these pages, PowerPoint has been installed as part of Office 2000 Standard. If you have a different version of Office, you may see slightly different things on your screen.

When you close all programs, the Windows® screen appears.

1. First, close any programs that are open. Find the CD-ROM drive on the system unit (see page 40). Press the button near the drive.

2. A drawer slides out. Place the CD-ROM in it, with the writing facing up. Press the button again, to close the drawer. Wait a moment.

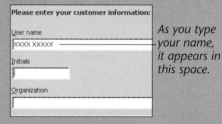

As you type your name, it appears in this space.

3. A box appears in the middle of the screen. Wait for a moment, while the computer gets ready to install the software.

4. The box changes. There are several white areas in the box. The insertion point is flashing in the white area below '*User name*'.

5. Type your name in the top white area. Now press the Tab key to move the insertion point into the second white area.

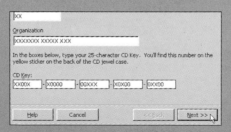

6. Type your initials, then press Tab. The insertion point is below '*Organization*'. Press Tab again, to move it to below '*CD Key*'.

7. Find the Product Key on the cover of your CD-ROM, and type it carefully. It fills the five white boxes as you type. Now click on *Next*.

8. A new box appears. Write down the number next to '*Product ID*', and keep it safe. You'll need it if you contact Microsoft® Technical Support.

Click here to read the rest of the End-User License Agreement.

Upgrade Now replaces Typical if an earlier version of Microsoft® Office is on your computer.

9. Now read the End-User License Agreement on the box. It tells you things that you need to know about using Microsoft® Office.

10. Once you have read the Agreement, click on the circle next to '*I accept the terms...*' so that a dot appears inside it. Now click on *Next*.

11. Another box appears. Click on *Typical*. If you have an earlier version of Office on your computer, you'll see *Upgrade Now*. Click on it.

12. A box pops up. Colour slowly fills the white area. After a while, a second box tells you that the computer will restart. Click on *Yes*.

13. The computer switches itself off and then back on again. A box appears. When colour fills the white area, PowerPoint is installed.

14. Now take the CD-ROM out of the drawer and put it back in its case. To start using Microsoft® PowerPoint 2000, turn to pages 6-7.

After installing

Once you've installed Microsoft® PowerPoint 2000 onto your computer, it's ready to use. However, first of all you need to fill in the Registration Card, which is in the box that Microsoft® Office 2000 came in. When you've filled it in, send it to Microsoft, to let them know that you've installed PowerPoint on your computer. You'll find the address of Microsoft in your country in one of the leaflets in the software box.

As you're installing software, don't worry if you have to wait for a while for each new screen to appear or if your computer makes funny noises. This is quite normal.

Troubleshooting

As you read this book, things may not always appear on your screen as you expect. Don't worry – these tips will help you out of any confusion.

Finding PowerPoint

This menu pops up when you click on Start.

Each tiny arrow links to another menu.

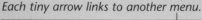
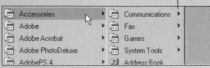

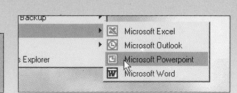

1. If you are trying to open PowerPoint 2000, but can't find it on the second menu that pops up when you start, you may still have it.

2. Click on the first item on the second menu with a tiny arrow next to it. Another menu appears. Check to see if PowerPoint is there.

3. If it is, click on it, if not, click on each item on the menu with an arrow beside it. If you still can't find it, it probably isn't installed yet.

Finding a missing toolbar

A toolbar is missing from here.

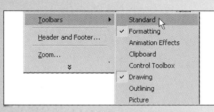

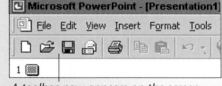

A toolbar now appears on the screen.

1. If you can't see all the toolbars you need, click on *View* then on *Toolbars*. Another menu appears.

2. *Standard*, *Formatting* and *Drawing* should all have a tick next to them. If one of these isn't ticked, click on it.

3. The menu disappears. The missing toolbar is now shown on your screen ready for you to use.

Fonts

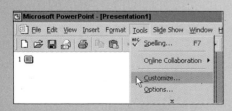

Options

A tick appears in the box when you click here.

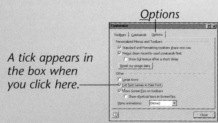

Click here to see the list of fonts.

1. If the fonts on the list of fonts all look the same on your screen, click on *Tools* then on *Customize*.

2. A box pops up. Click on *Options*, then on *List font names in their font* so a tick appears, then click on *Close*.

3. Click on the down arrow next to the Font box. The list of fonts now shows what each one looks like.

The Office Assistant

The Office Assistant can help with any problems you encounter. To make it appear, click on the Help tool on the Menu bar.

Help tool

Your question appears here as you type.

Type a word or a question, then click on *Search*. The Assistant offers lots of options. Click on one to find out more. When you've found out what you need, click on the x in the top corner to close Help. The Assistant stays on the screen. To remove it, right-click on it so that a menu appears, then click on *Hide*.

If you leave the Office Assistant on your screen while you are working, it will offer shortcuts and tips which may be useful.

The Projector Wizard

When you connect a laptop to a projector, you may need help from the Projector Wizard to make sure they work properly together.

The Projector Wizard asks you a series of questions then gives you different instructions, depending on the makes of your computer and projector.

You may need to click on the double arrows at the bottom of the menu to see the Set up Show option.

1. Click on *Slide Show* on the Menu bar. A menu drops down. Move the pointer to *Set Up Show* and click on it.

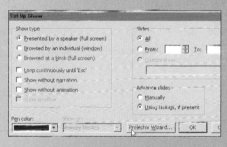

2. A box appears. Click on *Projector Wizard* near the bottom of the box to open the first page of the Wizard.

3. Answer the questions and follow the instructions on each page, then click on *Next* to go to the next page.

4. When you get to the final page, read the instructions carefully, then click on *Finish*. The projector is ready to use.

If the Projector Wizard can't help you, you'll need to check the projector's manual.

General troubleshooting

Computers can be baffling to a beginner, but don't worry if something unexpected happens while you're using your computer, there is usually a simple solution. Here are some tips for solving common problems.

1. If you leave your computer for a while, you may find that the screen goes blank, or fills with colours or patterns. Don't worry, just move the mouse and the screen will return to normal.

2. If you can't see Start in the bottom left-hand corner of the screen, try moving the pointer down to the very bottom of the screen. When it becomes a tiny black arrow, click and drag the pointer up. Start is dragged up with it.

3. If you think you may have lost a presentation, it may just be hidden under another one. Click on *Window* at the top of the screen. A menu drops down with a list of all the presentations that are open. Move the pointer over the name of the one you want, then click to make it appear.

4. If you accidentally double-click on a picture, a message appears asking if you want to change it to a Microsoft Office drawing object. Click on *No* to keep working.

5. If the first letter of a line of text turns into a capital letter, you can change it to a little letter by moving the insertion point to the right of the letter. Press the Backspace key, then type the letter again.

6. If your printer isn't printing, make sure that it has enough paper and that it's switched on. If it still doesn't work, you'll need to look at the printer's instructions.

7. If you make a mistake, you can undo it by holding down Ctrl and pressing the Z key.

8. If you are finding it difficult to change the appearance of lettering, pictures or charts on your slides, make sure that they are selected. The computer will only change things that are selected.

9. If a small menu suddenly appears on the screen, you may have accidentally pressed the right mouse button. To make the menu disappear, move the pointer away from the menu and click with the left mouse button.

10. If you can see the Windows® screen around the edge of the PowerPoint screen, click on the Maximize tool in the top right-hand corner of the screen. This makes PowerPoint fill the whole screen.

Maximize tool

11. If you can't see the PowerPoint screen, it may just be hidden. If *Microsoft PowerPoint* appears in a rectangle near the bottom of the screen, click on it to make the PowerPoint screen appear.

Click here to make PowerPoint appear.

Microsoft PowerPoint - [Pr...

12. If you type some words and they appear somewhere unexpected, this is because your insertion point is in the wrong place. Words you type always appear right next to the insertion point, wherever it is.

Glossary

Animation is a way to make words and pictures move.

A **bullet** is a dot that marks each new point on a typed list.

A **CD-ROM** is a kind of disc that is used to transfer programs onto a computer.

Clicking is pressing and quickly releasing the left mouse button.

Clicking and dragging is pressing and holding down the left mouse button, then moving the mouse.

Clip Art are pictures which come with PowerPoint. You can use them to illustrate your slides.

A **column chart** is a way to show information that compares several rows or columns of numbers.

A **datasheet** is a table you fill with numbers to create a column chart.

Double-clicking is pressing down and releasing the left mouse button twice, very quickly.

A **file name** is the name you give a presentation when you save it.

A **folder** is where you store presentations, pictures and any work created on a computer.

A **font** is a style of lettering.

Handles are tiny squares that appear around a selected picture, chart, table or text box.

Handouts are small versions of slides printed onto paper.

The **hard disk drive** stores folders and the programs that make the computer work.

Hardware is another name for computer equipment.

Importing means bringing a picture, created in a different program, into PowerPoint.

The **insertion point** is a small flashing line, which shows where typing will appear.

When you **install** software, it is loaded onto a computer, by transferring information from a CD-ROM onto the hard disk drive. Once this is done, the information stays there for you to use.

A **menu** is a list of options to choose from.

The **mouse** is used to move the pointer around the screen.

Notes are printed sheets to remind you what to say and do during a presentation.

Panes are the different sections of the PowerPoint window. It is usually divided into three panes.

The **pointer** is moved around the screen using the mouse. It usually looks like a small white arrow.

Programs give a computer instructions. PowerPoint is a computer program that comes as part of the Microsoft® Office group of programs.

Resizing is a way to make objects on slides bigger or smaller.

Right-clicking is pressing down and quickly releasing the right mouse button.

Saving is storing a presentation, or other work, on a computer.

Selecting words, pictures, tables or charts enables you to change their appearance.

Shutting down is the process you need to go through before switching a computer off.

A **slide** is a single page from a PowerPoint presentation.

A **slide show** is when all the slides of a presentation are shown one by one, in order.

Software is another name for computer programs.

A **system unit** contains the parts of the computer that store and process information.

A **table** is a way to arrange information in rows and columns.

Text is another name for words.

A **text box** is a box you type into to add words to a slide.

Tools are tiny pictures that you click on to tell the computer to do something. They are usually arranged in rows called toolbars.

Toolbars are lines of tools, grouped together.

A **transition** is a special effect for turning one slide into the next during a presentation.

Views are different arrangements of the PowerPoint window. The views used in this book are Normal View and Slide Sorter View.

A **window** is a box on the computer screen. Each new presentation or program opens in a new window.

Index

First published in 2002 by Usborne Publishing Ltd., 83-85 Saffron Hill, London, EC1N 8RT, England. www.usborne.com Copyright © 2002, Usborne Publishing Ltd.
The name Usborne and the devices ⚐ ⊕ are Trade Marks of Usborne Publishing Ltd. All rights reserved. No part of this publication may be reproduced, stored in a retrieval system or transmitted in any form or by any means, electronic, mechanical, photocopying, recording or otherwise, without prior permission of the publisher. Printed in Spain.
Managing editor: Fiona Watt Managing designer: Russell Punter With thanks to Henry Brook and Zoe Wray.